10 Women
POLITICAL PIONEERS

by Carol J. Perry

illustrations by Dick Smolinski

Published by Worthington Press
801 94th Avenue North, St. Petersburg, Florida 33702

Printed in the United States of America

2 4 6 8 10 9 7 5 3 1

ISBN 0-87406-642-5

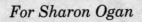

For Sharon Ogan

Contents

Introduction

Each of the ten women in this book is truly a pioneer in the world of politics. We know that a pioneer is someone who ventures into unknown new territories. The field of politics has been an unknown territory for women for centuries, but each of these women—working within the existing political system of her own country—has found ways to make a difference in the lives of her people.

These women are all recognized as leaders. Their names are known the world over. What do these ten women, from different cultures, different races, different family backgrounds, have in common? What is it that makes a woman a leader . . . a pioneer?

It isn't money or beauty. Only two of these women came from wealthy families. At least three were born into poverty. Most were from the middle class. Some of them were quite pretty. One was considered homely. Most were average-looking. Some of them were raised by both parents, some came from single-parent homes, and one was an orphan. Nine of them married and had children. All of them—rich or poor—managed to get a good education. All of them faced rejection and failure not just once, but many times. All of them had the support of other people who believed they could achieve their goals.

How can you become a pioneer? No one can tell you that exactly. But maybe reading about women who actually became political leaders in their own countries will give you some ideas you can use in your own life.

Corazon Aquino

"I have been kissed by the poorest of the poor and have felt the warmth of their tears on my cheeks . . . I cannot shut my ears to them. I cannot turn my back on them."

—Corazon Aquino

Corazon Cojuango, her three sisters and four brothers, all grew up on the Cojuango family's plantation on Luzon, the largest of 7,100 islands in the Republic of the Philippines. Corazon, whose full name was Maria Corazon Cojuango, was born there in 1933. The young girl, who was often called Cory, thought her island home was a very beautiful place. There were broad plains and sloping mountains. There were lakes and streams, and even a cone-shaped volcano.

Acres of sugarcane plants grew tall on the Cojuango plantation. Sometimes, workers harvesting the cane with big hooked knives would give Cory and her brothers and sisters little sections of the sweet, bamboo-like cane to eat. Cory loved her island home. Her brothers and sisters were her best friends and favorite playmates.

Cory's family was quite wealthy. And like many wealthy people in the Philippines, the Cojuango family was very interested in politics. Cory's father and her uncle both served their country as congressmen, and her grandfather had once run for the office of vice president.

There isn't any common language spoken in the Philippine Islands. In fact there are about eighty different languages and dialects spoken there. But almost everyone speaks a language called *Pilipino*, and English is taught in all of the public and private schools. Cory was good at learning languages, and she liked going to her private Catholic school in Manila, the modern capital city of the Philippines.

Because of the wealth and importance of the Cojuango family, Cory and the other children were invited to many parties and celebrations. Once, when Cory was around eight years old, she was invited to a birthday party at the home of another famous Filipino family, the Aquinos. There she met a boy her own age named Benigno Aquino, known as "Ninoy" to his family and friends.

"I think Ninoy liked you, Cory," teased her sister Josephine. "What do you think of him?"

"I think he's bratty," said Cory, remembering how Ninoy had boasted that he was a year ahead of her in school even though they were the same age.

Still, Cory saw Ninoy at parties from time to time as they grew up. Then Cory went to the United States to attend high school. After graduating from high school, she enrolled at Mount St. Vincent College in New York, a Roman Catholic school, where she majored in French and math.

Meanwhile, Benigno Aquino had become a successful journalist. He had become known around the world as a seventeen-year-old Korean War correspondent. One summer, when Cory was home from college, they met once again. Ninoy no longer seemed like a brat. Before long the two were exchanging love letters.

After graduation from St. Vincent, Cory went home

to Luzon. When she was about 26 years old, she and Ninoy were married. Cory wore a beautiful white silk gown embroidered with lace and jewels. The best man at the wedding was Ninoy's classmate and friend, Salvador Laurel.

It wasn't long before Ninoy became active in politics, and it was easy to see that this was something he was very good at. He quickly became the youngest mayor in the country's history. Then he became the youngest governor. Then, the youngest senator. Soon people were talking about the possibility of Benigno Aquino becoming the youngest president of the Philippines.

But Cory preferred a quiet life to a public one. She became a homemaker and mother, and as the years went by, Cory and Ninoy had five children. Cory was busy, indeed. But even though she preferred to remain in the background, she had a very real concern for the Philippines and the people who lived there. She worried about the way the country was being run by its president, Ferdinand Marcos. Many people believed that Marcos was dishonest. They also feared that he would destroy the people's freedom, making it impossible for democracy to exist in the Philippines. Ninoy and Cory thought that this was probably the sad truth.

President Marcos knew that Ninoy was thinking about running for president in the 1973 election. He also knew that Ninoy, with his good record in politics, would probably win in a fair election. To make sure this couldn't happen, Marcos insisted that the country be placed under martial law—temporary rule by the army to control citizens of the country.

It wasn't long before soldiers began to arrest people. Ninoy was among the first put in jail while Marcos

11

remained president. For nearly eight years, Ninoy was confined to a jail cell. Cory visited him almost every day, sometimes carrying messages to him from his friends.

When at last President Marcos said there would be an election in 1978, Ninoy decided to run for a seat in the Assembly, a law-making group something like the United States Congress. But since Ninoy was still in jail, other people had to make political speeches for him, including Cory.

Although Cory had never tried speaking in front of groups before, she began to speak in public. She told people what a good man her husband was. "Ninoy's love of country was only the other face of his love for God," Cory told them in one of her speeches. "And I think this is the truest and best kind of patriotism."

The Aquino children began to speak at political rallies too. President Marcos heard about this and didn't like it at all. He said that if Cory was a good mother, she wouldn't allow her children to do that. Cory sent back a message to the President: "The children will stop campaigning when their father is released from prison." But Ninoy was still not released.

Before the election was held, Ninoy had a heart attack. He needed an operation that could only be done in the United States. He was finally allowed out of jail to fly to Texas for surgery. The whole Aquino family went with him.

Ninoy's operation was a success, and the Aquinos moved to Massachusetts. Ninoy was asked to speak at several universities near Boston. Cory was happy to stay at home once again, and go back to being a wife and mother.

But after a while, Ninoy formed a plan to overthrow

the Marcos government. He felt that he had to return to the Philippines despite rumors that he would be assassinated if he returned. Ninoy didn't believe that would happen. Cory prayed that it wouldn't. They both knew that, at the very least, there was a good chance he would be arrested again.

When Benigno Aquino arrived at Manila International Airport, soldiers boarded the plane and escorted him off. Other soldiers prevented reporters and friends from following as Aquino made his way down the steps. Suddenly, a loud gunshot broke the silence and a moment later Ninoy lay dead on the runway.

Cory and the children flew to Manila right away. Cory was proud that two million people marched in Ninoy's funeral procession!

Months went by, and Cory began to realize that most of Ninoy's loyal friends were now looking to her for leadership. The small, quiet woman who was happiest at home with her children was suddenly being asked to continue her husband's fight to return democracy and freedom to their homeland.

Elections were planned for May 1984. People automatically assumed that the votes wouldn't be counted properly. President Marcos's people had ways of changing the results of the balloting so that their side always seemed to win. Some people wanted to boycott the elections. That is, they wanted people to stay home and refuse to vote at all. But Cory didn't agree. She encouraged everyone to vote. There were so many people who did as she asked that one-third of the assembly seats were won by candidates opposed to President Marcos.

In the Philippines, as in England, the party in power can call for an election even when one isn't regularly scheduled. It's called a "snap" election. President Marcos called for one to take place in February of 1986. He figured that because several different candidates would be running against him, the votes would be split up and he would win easily. But the opposition fooled him. They narrowed the field to one candidate—Cory Aquino.

Cory wasn't sure this was the right thing to do, but she thought about it and prayed about it for several days. Finally she decided that it was God's will that she should run for president. And she knew that President Marcos would not give up his power without a terrible fight. Cory prepared for the battle.

Salvador Laurel, a close friend of Ninoy's and best man at Cory's wedding, was a well-known Filipino who had been planning to run for president for a long time. He had a well-organized political party known as UNIDO to back him. Cory and Laurel talked things over. Without Laurel's political connections, Cory couldn't win. Without Cory's great popularity with the people, Laurel couldn't win. They decided to run as a team: Cory for president and Laurel for vice president.

To prevent the cheating on vote counts that everyone feared, they organized a citizen's committee called The National Movement for Free Elections (NAMFREL) to watch over the voting. Thousands of volunteers watched carefully as ballots were counted. The United States sent observers to help make sure the election was honest. By NAMFREL's count, Corazon Aquino won the election by 800,000 votes!

But President Marcos still wasn't ready to give up his power. Ignoring the election results, he announced to the National Assembly that *he* was the winner! Some assembly members got up and walked out.

Cory declared that *she* was the winner. She told the newspapers, "This is my message to Mr. Marcos and his puppets. Do not threaten Cory Aquino, because I am not alone."

Cory and Laurel invited their supporters to a huge rally, and more than a million people attended. Then they heard that some of the military leaders in the government were planning a revolt against Marcos. The leaders of that revolt were Defense Minister Juan Ponce Enrile and Lieutenant General Fidel V. Ramos. Hundreds of thousands of people, including rebel soldiers, supported them and gathered in the streets near the army camps.

Marcos ordered tanks to attack the rebels. People sat down in the streets or knelt and prayed as the tanks rushed toward them. But the soldiers whom Marcos had ordered to attack refused to fire on their own people and turned around.

On February 25, 1986, *two* presidential inaugurations took place! Cory's inauguration was broadcast over a television station that the rebel troops had taken over. Marcos's inauguration was supposed to be broadcast over the only TV station Marcos still controlled. But just as he stood in front of the cameras, rebel soldiers destroyed the transmission signal.

Before the day was over, Ferdinand Marcos and his family fled the grand presidential palace where they had lived for twenty years. The man who had ruled the Philippines for so long took a helicopter to find safety in Hawaii.

Cory Aquino was at last the official president of the Philippines. "I am sure that Ninoy is smiling at us now from the life after," she said in her first speech. "For we have truly proved him correct: the Filipino is worth dying for."

Cory's first act as president was to free all the political prisoners who had been put in jail by Marcos, just as Ninoy had been. Then she turned her attention to the many serious problems her country was facing.

Unemployment was high. Many people were very poor. The nation was deeply in debt. Several organizations threatened the peace. Cory called for a new constitution to replace the one Marcos had prepared. "It is for our children," she told the people, "so that they can live in freedom, so that we shall never have another dictator."

On February 2, 1987, a new constitution became law. It said that Cory would remain in office until 1992. Civil rights were guaranteed to everyone.

Cory refused to live in the grand palace left by Marcos. It was her hope that the money the Marcos family had kept for themselves could somehow be returned to the people of her country. She wanted her government to be able to provide opportunities for all citizens to have jobs and decent places to live. She wanted the rich farmlands to be more evenly divided so that more people could make money from the crops. Cory had very high hopes for the future of the Philippines.

After six years had passed, some things had become better for the people. Some of the money that Marcos and his followers were accused of stealing was eventually recovered. But it was not nearly enough to make much difference to the many poor Filipinos.

Cory's government also tried to make life easier in other ways. For example, it tried to make the process of getting building permits easier, faster, and cheaper. But because there was still too much "red tape" involved, many foreign investors who might have built factories in the Philippines went to other countries.

Cory knew that she had done her very best, but after her term was up she decided not to run for president again. Instead, she gave her support to Fidel V. Ramos, an old friend who had stood by her when Ferdinand Marcos had tried to claim victory in the 1986 election.

Even though Cory's peaceful overthrow of the Marcos dictatorship was praised by people all over the world, she refused to take credit for it. "The victory of the revolution does not belong to me," she said. "It belongs to the Filipino people."

Geraldine Ferraro

AN IMPORTANT FIRST

"We've chosen the path to equality. Don't let them turn us around."

—Geraldine Ferraro

Antonetta Ferraro was going to have a baby, and she was very worried. She and her husband Dominick had already had three babies—all of them boys—and two of them had died. One had only lived to be a week old, and three-year-old Gerard had been killed in an automobile accident.

Antonetta told Dominick that she was afraid to leave Carl, their remaining son, when she went to the hospital to have the baby. She was afraid something bad might happen to him while she was away. So Geraldine Ferraro was born at home on August 26, 1935, in a small, tidy house in Newburgh, New York.

The little baby girl made Antonetta and Dominick smile again. Their bad luck seemed to be changing. Dominick's restaurant and his store were doing well, and both of the children were healthy and happy. Everyone called the baby Gerry. She was a good-natured child, and she and her brother Carl loved playing with their dad. Gerry laughed and giggled when Dominick carried her piggyback up the stairs to her bedroom, even when she was a big third-grader.

Then one morning everything changed. When Gerry

and Carl woke up there was a doctor in their parents' bedroom. "What's wrong?" Gerry cried, rushing to the bed where her dad lay very still. He looked at her for a moment, then closed his eyes. Her mother took her hand and led her out of the room. "Daddy's gone to heaven," she said.

The sudden death of her father was almost more than Gerry could bear. Her father hadn't told anyone that he had a heart condition, and Gerry felt guilty about all those piggyback rides, thinking perhaps she had caused his heart attack. She felt terrible. She was only eight years old, and her whole life had changed overnight.

Antonetta was alone now, with two children to raise. The first thing that must be done, she decided, was to sell the house. She knew that without Dominick's income she couldn't afford to make house payments. She was too proud to ask anyone for help, and she was determined to do what was right for Gerry and Carl. As soon as the house was sold, the family moved to a tiny apartment in New York's South Bronx.

Gerry began to learn right away how important it is for men and women to know how to take care of themselves. Antonetta was very skillful at needlework, so to support the family she crocheted fancy beads onto beautiful dresses for women who could afford such things. She urged the children to study hard, to learn, and to never quit, no matter how difficult things got.

"Don't forget your name," she told her daughter. "*Ferro* means iron. You can bend it, but you can't break it."

Antonetta worked hard, and Gerry studied hard. Later, when she talked about that time of her life, Geraldine Ferraro said, "My father's death changed my life forever. I found out how quickly what you have can be taken away. From that moment on, I had to fight for whatever I wanted, to work and study my own way out of the South

Bronx and take my mother with me."

Gerry's mother wanted very much for her children to be able to attend college. She must have been very pleased and proud when Gerry won a full scholarship to Marymount Manhattan College. Still, Antonetta had to keep working just as hard as ever. There were books and materials and clothes to buy even though Gerry was working part-time to help with her own expenses.

"What are you knocking yourself out for, sending her to college?" wondered one of Geraldine's uncles. "She's pretty. She'll get married."

"Forget it," Antonetta told him sharply. "She's going to have an education."

By the time Gerry graduated from Marymount, she knew that what she really wanted to do was study law. So, during the day she taught English to children, and in the evening she went to law school. She was one of only three women in her class to graduate. All the hard work and extra studying seemed worthwhile when Gerry passed her New York state bar exam, the difficult written test that must be passed in order to practice law.

But the uncle who had predicted that Gerry would get married was right too. The same week that she became a lawyer, Geraldine Ferraro married businessman John Zaccaro. She kept the name Ferraro, though. She said, "I wanted to pay public tribute to my mother . . . for all she had done for me. That's why I kept her name professionally after I got married, to honor her."

Gerry and John had agreed that once they had children Gerry would stay at home with them until they were all in school full time. They had three children— Donna, Laura, and John, Jr. So it wasn't until fourteen years later, in 1974, that Gerry went to work for the District Attorney's office in Queens, New York.

21

It wasn't easy to change from being a full-time mother to being a full-time attorney. Many laws had changed over the years and Geraldine had to study all over again. But before long she was handling forty cases at a time. "After a while," she said, "your mind just expands to hold what it has to know."

In 1977 she was promoted to bureau chief, which meant that she had to work very closely with all sorts of crime victims. She saw that more help was needed for people who weren't able to fully take care of themselves, including old people, poor mothers and their children, and people who couldn't read or write. She wanted to make a difference in their lives, and the best way to do that, it seemed to her, was to run for election to the United States Congress.

Gerry felt that people should feel free to walk into a congressional representative's office anytime they felt like it and find someone there who could talk to them or help them. When she won the congressional election in 1978, the first thing she did was open an office just like that in the Queens district of New York where she lived. She made sure that there were no steps because she wanted handicapped people to be able to get in easily. She didn't even have blinds or curtains on the windows because she wanted people walking by to look in and see the work going on.

Gerry wanted to learn all she could about what was happening in Congress in order to best represent the people who had elected her to such a high office. She became a regular visitor at the Library of Congress. She read and studied and researched. Before long she was as comfortable in Congress as she was back in her office in New York. When Congress wasn't in session in Washington, D.C., Gerry would plan "town meetings" in

Queens so that the people she represented could come and tell her about their problems.

The people in Queens liked the way their congresswoman worked for them. They elected her three times. Meanwhile, Geraldine was becoming quite well-known in Washington, too. She was known as a fighter, as someone who would press hard for a cause she believed in.

One of the things Geraldine believed was that Walter Mondale would make a good president of the United States. Mondale had served in the United States Senate for two terms. Then he had been vice president of the United States when Jimmy Carter was president. Gerry wanted to help Mondale get the Democratic Party's nomination. She made speeches telling people what a good president Mondale would make. She was pleased when it turned out that Walter Mondale was chosen to run for president on the Democratic ticket in 1984.

The person who has been nominated by a political party for the office of president usually selects the person who will run for the office of vice president. Some experts predicted Mondale would choose a woman to be the vice-presidential candidate. No woman in the history of the United States had ever been nominated for this high office. Everyone wondered which of the well-known women in the Democratic Party might be the one chosen. Would it be the outspoken congresswoman from Colorado, Pat Schroeder? Congresswoman Barbara Mikulski of Maryland? Perhaps then-mayor of San Francisco Dianne Feinstein? Former Congresswoman Barbara Jordan of Texas? And what about Congresswoman Geraldine Ferraro from New York?

Gerry was invited to Walter Mondale's house for an interview. It lasted three hours. She answered questions about her views on many issues facing the United States.

The two talked about crime, about the economy, and about America's involvement with other countries. Gerry couldn't tell whether Mondale approved of her or not. But either way, she planned to work very hard for him in his campaign against President Ronald Reagan.

Then came the telephone call from Mondale. "Will you be my running mate?" he asked.

"That would be terrific," said Gerry. One of the first people she called with the news was her mother. "Of course it would be you," said Antonetta. "I've known it all along. Who could be a better vice president?"

Suddenly, Gerry found herself the center of attention as never before. Cameras and television lights seemed to be everywhere. Police held back crowds in front of her hotel. "Who are those people waiting for? Who's coming in?" she asked on one occasion.

"You," was the reply.

"Me?" She could hardly believe it. People everywhere wanted to see for themselves the first woman in America to run for the office of vice president.

Finally, the night of Gerry's nomination arrived. She wore her favorite white dress. She had rehearsed what she was going to say to the huge crowd in the convention hall, and to the even bigger audience watching on TV. She especially wanted to thank her mother for all the support and love she had given Gerry over the years.

Geraldine Ferraro's speech began, "Tonight, the daughter of a woman whose highest goal was a future for her children talks to our nation's oldest party about a future for us all."

The delegates to the Democratic convention rose to their feet and cheered. They whistled and stamped their feet. It was a wonderful night for Gerry and her family.

Gerry learned soon after the convention that running

for such a high office wasn't easy. Some newspapers printed stories about her family that made her very sad. They said that her husband John did business with criminals. They even wrote about her father, who had died so long ago, and said that he had been in jail once.

But Geraldine Ferraro remembered what her mother had told her about *Ferro* meaning "iron." She promised herself that she wouldn't break, no matter what. "These things are not true," Gerry said, and went right on campaigning.

All over the United States, Gerry made speeches and shook hands with voters, and told them what Walter Mondale would do if he were elected. She told them how she felt about controlling nuclear weapons to make the world safer. She told them how worried she was about millions of Americans without jobs. She asked them to think about cleaning up the environment. She talked about the many women who were raising families alone, and about the needs of America's older people. She tried her best to convince everyone that the United States would be better off with Walter Mondale as president, and Geraldine Ferraro as his vice president. Sometimes, she flew in and out of as many as five states in one day!

When election day arrived on November 6, 1984, Gerry was glad the campaign was over. She knew that—win or lose—she had done her very best.

Walter Mondale and Geraldine Ferraro did not win the presidential election. But Geraldine knew that the very fact that she had been courageous and confident enough to run for this high office meant a lot to many people. When she gave the newspapers and television stations her statement conceding the election to the Republicans she said: "We fought hard. We gave it our best. We did what was right. And we made a difference."

Indira Gandhi

MADAME PRIME MINISTER

"I am not a person to be pressured—by anybody or any nation."

—Indira Gandhi

It was a warm January afternoon in 1966 when Indira Gandhi stood on the front lawn of her small home and faced her first press conference as prime minister of India. There were 500 million people living in the sprawling South Asian country when she took office. That made the tall, dark-eyed widow the head of the largest democracy in the world.

But India had not always had a form of government in which leaders of the country were elected by the people. In fact, when Indira was born in 1917 to Jawaharlal and Kamala Nehru, India was still part of the British Empire. The people of India were ruled by people from England.

Fortunately, little Indu, as she was often called at home, had been born into a fairly wealthy family. In a land where many children barely had enough to eat, the Nehru home was full of delicate works of art and the good smells of Indian cooking.

There were fine horses in the stables, gentle enough for a small girl to ride. Gardens were bright with flowers and sweet-smelling fruit trees. On hot days—and it is

27

often very hot in India—Indu played in a special "summerhouse." The summerhouse had pools, and fountains that splashed among blossoms and stone statues.

Sometimes Indu went on summer holidays with her parents to a vacation home. The home was high in the hills, far away from the heat and noise of the city. They would return home in the fall, in time for Indira's November birthday and for the Diwali festival, a traditional Indian festival of lights. The Nehru house would have hundreds of miniature oil lamps on every window sill and balcony. It must have looked like an enchanted palace from a fairy tale.

Indira's father Jawaharlal and her grandfather Motilal were very interested in politics. Both men were lawyers and understood how governments work. They knew how very serious India's problems were. They believed that political change was needed, and needed soon. Millions of Indians were unhappy living under British rule. People could be arrested without warning and put in jail without trial. They began to protest with strikes and riots. Jawaharlal Nehru and his family began to work for the day when India would be independent—free to rule herself.

So it turned out that Indira Nehru's peaceful childhood changed suddenly into a strange world of political meetings on the lawn, police knocking on the door day and night, and relatives going to prison. Indira's father and grandfather stopped wearing pin-striped suits and silk neckties. They began to wear *khadi,* coarse white homespun robes. They put away their shining black top hats and wore simple white cloth caps instead.

Even though Indira understood that wearing the simpler garments showed support for Indian custom, she didn't like giving up her beautiful clothes. But she obeyed her parents and learned to wear the scratchy, heavy khadi. She learned to hold her head high, even when her father and grandfather were taken to jail for defying British laws.

Then, when the Nehrus refused to pay fines the British court said they owed, the police returned to take carpets and furniture out of the house in payment. The officers laughed as little Indu stamped her tiny feet and tried to chase them away. But it wasn't one bit funny to Indira. Her secure world had been invaded by uniformed enemies, and she would never forget it.

That was just the beginning. Jawaharlal and his father were arrested many times. The family settled into a routine of prison visits and prison letters. For a long period of time the whole family lived a topsy-turvy life.

Once, when Indira was eleven, her father even came home cut and bleeding. He had been leading a peaceful protest that had been broken up by police. The police had beaten the demonstrators with long, metal-tipped poles. But the family's political efforts were being felt. Just two weeks after the beating, the whole family cheered and scattered flower petals from a balcony as grandfather Motilal Nehru rode past in a grand carriage drawn by thirty-four white horses. He had been elected president of the Indian National Congress. Although the organization had no real power in government, it was an important voice in the Indian struggle for freedom.

The very next year it was Indira's father who was elected president of the Congress. When her grandfather turned the office over, Jawaharlal rode through the streets on a great white horse. People tossed flowers from windows and rooftops as he passed.

Perhaps the scene looked like a picture from a

storybook, but Indira knew that the Nehru family didn't live in a make-believe world. Unrest in India continued to grow. More and more people disobeyed British rules. Thousands of Indians were taken to crowded and dirty prisons. Once again, Indira's father was jailed. Before long her grandfather and her uncle were arrested too.

But something exciting was beginning to happen at the same time. As more and more men were taken to jail, some Indian women began to get involved in politics. This was unusual because most Indians still observed *purdah*—a kind of seclusion of women. For instance, a woman ate only after her husband had finished. She remained silent while men spoke. Marriages were arranged by parents.

But some women, especially those with good educations and wealth, had increasingly become used to a certain amount of freedom. Now they began to speak out. The women of Indira's family moved into the front lines of India's political struggle. They addressed meetings and organized parades. They picketed shops so that foreign goods couldn't be sold.

There was plenty for children to do too. By the time Indira was twelve, she was leading a group called the Children's Brigade. She wore trousers and a khadi tunic, with a round cap perched at an angle on her shiny dark hair. Grown-ups smiled and called the youngsters the "Monkey Army," but Indira and her friends took the matter very seriously. They drilled and marched, sometimes before dawn. They picketed shops. They even sewed bright red and green Congress flags and hung them boldly in public places.

The fight for India's future went on for years. Indira's father was in and out of prison. Her frail mother was in and out of hospitals. And Indira was in and out of schools. Sometimes she even had to arrange for her own schooling because everyone else was sick or in jail.

But she made it to college and studied at far-away Oxford University in England. There, she met an old friend from home, a young man named Feroze Gandhi. The Nehru family was not exactly happy when Indira announced that she and Feroze were to be married. Feroze was not a follower of the Hindu religion, but that didn't seem to bother the Nehrus as much as the fact that he was quite poor.

It didn't matter to Indira. She had made up her mind. For her wedding she wore a simple pink cotton sari with fresh flowers in her hair. For the honeymoon, she chose a trip to the hills she had loved so much as a child. Then Indira and Feroze threw themselves wholeheartedly into their country's cause.

One day Indira was addressing a public meeting when the police came and arrested her. Feroze, who was watching from a window, jumped to her defense. He was promptly arrested too. For Indira, it was a proud moment. For most of her life she had seen her father, grandfather, mother, grandmother, aunts, and uncles go to jail. Now this strange honor was hers. She remained in jail for nearly a year, and a few months after her release, Feroze too was freed.

A year later the first of their two sons, Rajiv, was born. Indira's father was in prison again. But Jawaharlal Nehru was an important figure in or out of jail. By the time Indira's second son, Sanjay, arrived two years later, Jawaharlal Nehru was respected not only in India, but in many other countries. As his influence grew, there was more and more pressure for change in India.

Finally, on August 15, 1947, India was declared an independent nation. The country was free at last from British rule and looked to Indira's father to guide it as prime minister. Indira stayed politically active as well. She took over the duties of running her father's house. She joined him in his travels and was welcomed by famous leaders the world over.

Indira Gandhi had become an important and influential person in her own right. In 1955 she was invited to join the Congress Working Committee. Before long she joined the influential Parliamentary Board. Her power was growing.

Then, early in 1964, Nehru suffered a stroke. Indira took over many of his duties, but he died within a few months and a man named Lal Bahadur Shastri became prime minister. Only two years later, Shastri died too. Indira Gandhi was elected prime minister of India. It was an awesome responsibility. Poverty, hunger, ignorance, superstition, and disease plagued her beloved country.

In her white homespun sari and brown shawl, she stood before news reporters from all over the world. "How do you feel about being the first woman prime minister?" she was asked.

She drew herself up to her full height. Her dark eyes flashed. "I do not regard myself as a woman," she replied quietly. "I regard myself as a person with a job."

Governing India proved difficult indeed. People became more and more discontented with the way things were. Thousands of citizens who disagreed with Indira's plans for India were sent to prison. It was not the way Indira had envisioned India's future, and in 1977 she announced a general election. She believed that most of the people in India still agreed with her ideas about improving education, distributing food more fairly and punishing criminals and smugglers. She was sure she would be re-elected, but it wasn't to be. The Congress Party was defeated and she lost her seat in Parliament.

Even then, Indira would not turn her back on what she believed. In 1980 she promised the people that she would give them a better government and that she would make prices lower on things they wanted to buy. Her popularity in India grew again. Once more, she became prime minister.

But some Indian citizens known as Sikhs (pronounced *Seeks*) were very much opposed to her kind of government. Even though Indira did everything she knew to keep them from overthrowing her rule, they refused to obey the laws. Tension built steadily.

In the fall of 1984, Indira learned that the Sikhs were storing weapons and explosives in an important religious building known as The Golden Temple. She sent Indian soldiers to invade the temple and arrest the Sikh leaders headquartered there. This made the Sikhs very angry. Indira knew she was in danger, but she had faced danger before. As always, she went about her business calmly.

Her business was never to be completed. As she walked through her garden later that year, Indira was shot and killed by Sikh members of her own security guard. They were men she had known and trusted for many years.

When the Indian people learned what had happened, terrible riots broke out and hundreds of Sikhs were attacked and their homes burned. Indira's son Rajiv became the new prime minister. His first order of business was restoring order to the country that his mother had loved so much.

Barbara Jordan

"What the people want is very simple. They want an America as good as its promise. That's what they want."

—Barbara Jordan

It couldn't have been easy growing up poor and black in Houston, Texas back in the 1930s. Barbara Charline Jordan was born there in 1936, the youngest of the Reverend Benjamin and Arlynne Jordan's three daughters.

In those days black people in Texas were not allowed to go to the same schools or even eat at the same lunch counters as white people. Barbara's parents knew that the only way for their daughters to get ahead was to get a good education. Barbara's father used to tell his daughters, "No one can ever take away your brains!"

Barbara's grandparents were important in her growing-up years too. Barbara's family shared their neat pink house with her Grandfather and Grandmother Jordan. But the family always spent Sundays after church with her other grandparents, the Pattens.

Barbara's grandfather John Ed Patten was in the junk business, and on Sunday afternoons Barbara would go into the yard with him and help bundle rags and old newspapers and scrap metal. Her grandfather always gave Barbara part of the money he earned when he sold the junk.

Grandfather Patten's influence was felt in other ways, too. He was particular about the kids Barbara played with. "You don't have to be like those others," he told her. "You just trot your own horse and don't get into the same rut as everyone else." He was proud of his family, and he often told Barbara about his father, who was a lawyer in Washington. Barbara was just a little girl and didn't know exactly what a lawyer was, but she liked the sound of it.

Barbara's mother, Arlynne, was well-known as a speaker in various Baptist churches in the Houston area. Barbara felt proud whenever she heard her mother give a warm, welcoming speech at a Baptist convention. Barbara's father, Ben, had attended Tuskegee Institute, a well-known Alabama college. Not only had he been a good student, but he had been on the football team as well. He devoted much of his time to Bible study and was a popular preacher at the Good Hope Missionary Baptist Church.

There was always fun at the Jordan house even though there wasn't much money. Almost all of the members of the family played a musical instrument—Barbara's favorite was the guitar—and they were all good singers. Barbara and her sisters, Bennie and Rose Mary, sang together at different churches. They were known as The Jordan Sisters.

There were influences outside of the family, too. Barbara attended Phillis Wheatley High School, a segregated school named for a famous black poet. One of her favorite teachers was Mamie Reed Lee. Mamie Reed Lee liked to give the kids advantages they normally wouldn't have, such as bus trips to hear the Houston Symphony Orchestra. It was the sort of thing Barbara always remembered. Another thing she never forgot was a speech she heard in tenth grade. The speaker was a black lawyer visiting the area from Chicago. Barbara was impressed and made up her mind right then that she would be a lawyer too.

Since both of her parents spoke in public regularly, Barbara didn't find it unusual to be asked to speak in front of an audience. She often recited poetry in church. Teachers sometimes required students to memorize poems or pieces of literature and recite them aloud. Barbara enjoyed speaking in public and discovered that she was good at it.

Barbara and her sisters had always been encouraged to be outstanding, to be different . . . to do their best. Barbara aimed high, deciding that she wanted to be named Girl of the Year. This was an honor given by a national black sorority to the most outstanding girl in the senior class. She became very serious about succeeding in school. Debating became one of her favorite activities. She often won medals and trophies for local, regional, and district debates with students from other schools. The announcement she had hoped for came in her senior year. Barbara Jordan was selected as Girl of the Year.

Even then, Barbara set new goals. She continued to get better and better at public speaking. Her debate coach suggested that she enter some contests. Before long Barbara was invited to compete in a national competition. She won, and when a reporter asked her about the victory she said, "It's just another milestone I have passed; it's just the beginning."

Along with all the debating trophies and medals,

37

Barbara received some scholarship money. It came in handy when she became a pre-law student at Texas Southern University, an all-black school. Of course, Barbara immediately joined the debating team. Her coach, Tom Freeman, wanted the team to become known outside of the local community. He set up competitions with debaters from other cities. The team would pile into the coach's car and head for Chicago, Boston, or New York. Along the way, the debaters had to rely on restaurants that would serve blacks. But once they got to northern cities, restrictions were not a problem. Barbara and the others could go into restaurants through the front door and sit anywhere they liked.

Back home in Texas, some doors were beginning to open too. In 1954 when Barbara was a junior in college, the United States Supreme Court made an important ruling. In a famous case known as *Brown v. The Board of Education,* the court said that school segregation was wrong. Black and white children should attend school together.

Barbara was delighted. "Finally," she said, "those kids in elementary and high schools are going to be able to go to school with white kids, and that's going to be good. I wish it had happened a few years earlier so I could have been with those white kids myself, because I would have loved it."

Barbara began to have opportunities to test her debating skills against white speakers, one-on-one. She continued to win. She also realized that if she was going to succeed in an integrated world, her chances would improve if she attended an integrated law school instead of the still all-black Texas Southern University. Her coach suggested Boston University. Barbara sent for the catalogs and showed them to her father.

"This is where I want to go," she told him. As always, Barbara's father was encouraging. "If you want to go, we'll manage." he replied. Her sisters also offered to help by sending her twenty dollars a month from their salaries.

There were 600 freshmen law students in Barbara's class at Boston University. Only six were women. Only two were black women.

The challenge was huge. Boston University opened up a new and unfamiliar world to Barbara. She felt that she had missed a lot by attending segregated schools and believed that she would have to work harder than anyone else. She made a point of really thinking things through before reaching conclusions. Just being a good speaker was no longer good enough. "I had learned," Barbara said later, "that you couldn't just say a thing was so . . . because somebody smarter and more thoughtful would come out and tell you it wasn't so. Then, if you still thought it was, you had to prove it."

Her efforts paid off. Barbara graduated from Boston University in 1959 and returned to Texas. It was just about the time the civil rights movement was starting to get attention. The movement was a huge effort to guarantee that no American would be treated any differently from anyone else because of race or nationality or religion. Black and white people everywhere were working hard to end segregation, which many people recognized as wrong and unfair. Barbara wanted to use her abilities as a lawyer to help change things for black people.

The following year, 1960, was an election year. Barbara decided that maybe the best way to work for change was through politics. She volunteered to help in the presidential election campaign of John F. Kennedy and his vice presidential running mate, Lyndon B. Johnson of Texas. And what better way than by using the speaking skill she had so carefully practiced? Before long, Barbara was speaking to both black and white groups, clubs, and churches. By the time the Kennedy-Johnson campaign successfully finished, Barbara had been "bitten by the political bug." She began to think about running for office herself.

She had plenty of support. In 1962 friends encouraged Barbara to run for the Texas House of Representatives. She did, and she campaigned hard. In the end, though, she didn't win. Barbara tried again in 1964, and lost again. She began to wonder, "Is politics worth staying in for me?" She asked herself, "How many more times are you going to run, Barbara?" The answer was simple: "One more time."

In 1967 Barbara ran again, this time for the state senate. She beat her white male opponent two to one. Newspapers all over America wrote about the first black woman in the Texas Legislature. Her picture was even in *Time* magazine. Then Barbara quietly began to learn all she could about how exactly things worked in the Texas Legislature, and about how she could best serve the people who had elected her.

One day, after she'd been in office for about a month, she was surprised to receive an invitation to meet with President Lyndon Johnson. President Johnson had taken office after President Kennedy was assassinated. President Johnson wanted to uphold civil rights, and needed to talk to Barbara about a new fair housing law he was proposing.

The President was impressed with Barbara's thoughtful remarks. It was the beginning of a special friendship between the two Texans: one, the wealthy, powerful President of the United States, and the other, a young black woman from Houston's poorest neighborhood.

Barbara worked hard while she was in the state senate. She worked on laws to end discrimination and to give farm workers the right to earn a minimum wage. She became the most popular senator in Texas. So no one was surprised when Barbara announced that she was planning to run for the Congress of the United States.

President Johnson himself, now retired from public office, came to Barbara's first fund-raising dinner. He told the cheering crowd, "Barbara Jordan proved to us that black is beautiful before we knew what that meant. Wherever she goes, she is going to be at the top." He was right. Barbara was elected to the United States House of Representatives in 1972, the first black woman from a southern state ever to serve in Congress. The Texans in Washington gave Barbara a special reception party. But shortly after that Barbara learned that her good friend President Johnson had died, which brought sadness to the happy occasion.

Barbara had a lot to learn . . . again. There were so many members of Congress—435 of them. Barbara was used to a 31-member state senate. She spent hours studying, reading, trying to do her very best for the people of Texas. She became a member of the Congressional Black Caucus, a group of black legislators.

Barbara was especially interested in the Constitution. She felt that no one was above the law . . . the law had to work for all Americans. In 1974 she was a member of a committee that had to decide if the man who was then president, Richard Nixon, had covered up the fact that some of his assistants had broken the law in trying to get him elected. Barbara's powerful voice was heard on the radio and on TV during the committee's hearings. She explained that the committee thought the President could be charged with breaking the law of the land. President Nixon resigned and his vice president, Gerald Ford, took office.

Then in 1976, people all over America watched as Barbara Jordan gave what may have been the best speech of her life. She gave the keynote address at the Democratic convention, where Jimmy Carter was nominated to run for president. The great convention hall suddenly grew silent as Barbara talked about democracy, and what it meant that she, a black woman, had been given the honor of giving the address. The next day the *Houston Post* said, "A poor kid from Houston's Fifth Ward sealed her destiny as a national superstar." A lot of people thought Barbara would make a good candidate for vice president! But Barbara said, "No, thank you." She liked her job in Congress and wanted to stay there for a while.

In 1978, after serving for three two-year terms in the House of Representatives, Barbara retired from public office and returned to Texas. She went to work at the University of Texas in Austin, where she now teaches at the school named for her old friend—the Lyndon Baines Johnson School of Public Affairs. She continues to write and to lecture and is still one of America's most famous women. She spoke at the 1992 Democratic convention in New York City when Arkansas Governor Bill Clinton was nominated for president. Again, the vast convention hall grew silent as her strong voice rang out, and again, the people in the audience jumped to their feet cheering and applauding when she had finished.

Many people still say that Barbara Jordan should hold another important position in government someday. And perhaps she will. Her many friends and admirers won't be surprised. And neither would her Grandfather Patten—who taught her to "trot her own horse!"

UNITED STATES   UNITED K

Jeane J. Kirkpatrick

FIRST AMERICAN WOMAN AMBASSADOR TO THE U.N.

"The world is open for American women to participate in almost any kind of activity that they want to if they prepare themselves for it and work at it.

—Jeane J. Kirkpatrick

When Jeane Jordan was born in Duncan, Oklahoma in 1926, her parents, Leona and Welcher Jordan, were excited about the future. Oil and natural gas had been discovered in Oklahoma, and Welcher had dreams of making a major strike. He was what oil drilling crews called a "wildcatter." Sometimes the crews met up with real wildcats when they were exploring for oil. They shot the big cats, then hung the carcasses on their oil derricks. Soon people began calling those wells "wildcat wells," and the men who worked there—"wildcatters." To find oil the wildcatters used both scientific knowledge and hunches and intuition . . . "a little luck—and a lot of work."

Because of the way wildcatters worked, the Jordans moved around quite a lot in search of oil. But little Jeane didn't mind. Her mother kept her happily entertained with storybook after storybook. There were pets to play with too. Then, just eight days after Jeane's eighth birthday, her little brother Jerry was born. As he grew older they became great friends and playmates.

Jeane loved school and she was usually an A student. "I wasn't very good at P.E. though," she admitted. "It's the only thing I ever flunked!"

When Jeane finished high school in Mt. Vernon, Illinois, she enrolled at Stephens College in nearby Columbia, Missouri. She received a two-year degree from Stephens, then transferred to Barnard College in New York City. Barnard was the women's college of Columbia University. This was Jeane's first experience living alone in a big city. It was an exciting time.

Jeane had always been interested in writing, so she thought about studying journalism in college. "But I felt that I didn't know anything to write about, and I wanted to know more. I wanted to study the big ideas."

Jeane decided to study philosophy. She thought that she might like to become a university professor someday. "What I wanted to do," she explained, "was go on reading and thinking and learning."

World War II had ended and the United States, under President Harry Truman, was trying to combat communism. The more Jeane studied, the more convinced she was that the United States had to prevent the spread of a system that she said "tries to establish political control over the lives of individuals . . . claiming for the state the whole life of the whole people!" She supported President Truman's plan to aid countries like Greece and Turkey in their fight to keep from being swallowed up by communist nations. President Truman was a Democrat, Jeane's parents were Democrats, and as soon as Jeane turned twenty-one in 1947 and was old enough to vote, she became a Democrat too.

After she finished at Barnard, Jean studied political science at Columbia. Her interest in government led her to Washington, D.C. and the United States Department of State. She was hired there to analyze the history of America's economic aid to Europe after the war.

Jeane's careful, well-organized work was noticed by a senior political scientist named Dr. Evron Kirkpatrick, known as Kirk to his friends. Jeane began to work under his direction. Then in 1952, she received a grant to study at the University of Paris's Institute of Political Science. Jeane had studied French in both high school and college. This would give her a chance to become really fluent in the language and besides, it would allow her to learn more about one of her favorite hobbies—French cooking.

That winter her old boss, Kirk Kirkpatrick, happened to be in Paris. He called and invited her to lunch. Then they had a few dinners together. They found that they had a great deal in common. They were both political scientists. They were both Democrats. And Kirk loved Jeane's French cooking. In 1955, when Jeane was twenty-eight, they were married—and spent their honeymoon at a political science conference!

In 1956, the first of their three sons was born. Jeane decided to give up her full-time career to stay home with her little boys, Doug, John, and Stuart, until the youngest son started nursery school. But Jeane didn't give up research altogether. Between 1956 and 1962 she worked on a special project about a subject she'd always found interesting, "Communism in Government." She continued with her writing. More and more often, Jeane J. Kirkpatrick's name was found on articles in scholarly publications.

When all three of her boys were old enough to be in school, Jeane accepted a job teaching at Trinity College in Washington, D.C. In 1967 she became an associate professor of political science. It was the job she had dreamed about when she'd first started college. Kirk and the boys were proud of her. And through her writing, the name of Jeane J. Kirkpatrick was becoming familiar to people in government and in universities around the country.

In 1974 Jeane wrote a book called *Political Women,* and her work began to attract even more attention. The following year she was asked to serve on an important committee to help prepare for the 1976 Democratic National Convention. Senator Henry M. Jackson of Washington wanted to be the Democratic candidate for President of the United States. Jeane hoped that he would be nominated. But Senator Jackson wasn't nominated. Jimmy Carter was, so Jeane supported him.

After Carter became president, Jeane began to criticize his handling of foreign affairs. She wrote an article called "Dictatorships and Double Standards" that explained what she thought he was doing wrong: President Carter was friendly to governments that she thought were enemies of America, while he turned away from governments she thought were America's friends. Jeane and other Democrats who were worried about America's dealings with foreign governments had a meeting with President Carter to try to convince him to take a stronger position against the world's communist leaders. But President Carter didn't agree with them.

Ronald Reagan, who wanted the Republican nomination for president, read Jeane's article. He wrote to Jeane and told her it was the best article he had ever read on the subject. She called him to thank him. After they'd talked for a while, she decided to support him in his campaign for president. This was a very big step for

Jeane. She had always been a Democrat and now she was going to help a Republican get elected!

Jeane was an advisor to Ronald Reagan. She helped coach him for his campaign debates against Jimmy Carter. Reagan won the election by a large majority, and Jeane became one of his advisors on foreign policy.

One winter night in 1980 Kirk and Jeane were having dinner when Jeane got a message to call Ronald Reagan. "How are you?" Jeane asked the president.

"I'll be better," he replied, "if you agree to serve as our ambassador to the United Nations!"

It was a great honor. Jeane was the very first woman to head the United States delegation to the United Nations. It was not an easy job. She had to move to New York while Kirk remained at their home in Maryland. She got up at six-thirty in the morning and often worked all day and right through dinner at night. "There was zero time for myself," she said.

Jeane often made headlines as ambassador while she helped the United States influence world affairs. The United Nations faced many difficult problems during the years that Jeane was there. Israel invaded Lebanon. The United States took military action in Grenada. The Soviet Union shot down a Korean airliner. Jeane always expressed her views strongly. Sometimes her ideas were praised and sometimes they were criticized. She remained ambassador until she resigned in 1985 to teach at Georgetown University.

Jeane thinks that women today can successfully combine a career and marriage. "My experience demonstrates that it's possible for women in our times to successfully combine traditional and professional roles. All that is required is a little luck—and a lot of work!"

Wilma Mankiller

LEADER OF A NATION

*"It's like running a big corporation and a little country at
the same time."*

—Wilma Mankiller

Centuries ago, the American Indians known as the
Cherokee were a proud nation that spread out over much
of the Southeast. The Cherokee hunted, fished, and
farmed in an area that covered parts of eight of our
present states.

But by 1945, the year that Wilma Pearl Mankiller
was born in Adair County in Oklahoma to a Cherokee
father and a Dutch-Irish mother, that great Cherokee
nation was no more. The millions of acres of land that
had once belonged to the Cherokee were now part of the
United States of America.

Wilma's parents, Charlie and Irene Mankiller, were
hardworking farmers just as those long-ago Cherokees
had been. They taught Wilma and her ten brothers and
sisters how to plant, hoe, and harvest crops of plump,
juicy strawberries.

The Mankillers, who got their name from a Cherokee
warrior ancestor, didn't have running water or electricity
in their house. But they didn't feel poor. With so many
brothers and sisters, Wilma always had someone to play

with. The wooded hills around the farmhouse made a fine playground. And in the evening, Wilma's father liked to tell his children stories about the history and the legends of the Cherokee.

He told them about how the Cherokee people of long ago had hunted with bow and arrow for deer and bear. He showed them how to make canoes in the old way, by hollowing out a tree trunk and filling it with hot coals, then scraping the inside with sharp stones. He told sad stories about their ancestors too. The one that made Wilma feel like crying was the true story of "The Trail of Tears." It went like this:

Long ago, gold was found on Cherokee land in Georgia. People flooded onto the Indian land. All of them wanted gold. The state of Georgia demanded that the Indians get out. Even though the United States Supreme Court said that the land was rightfully theirs, President Andrew Jackson ordered the Cherokee to leave anyway, and settle in land west of the Mississippi River. Although many of the Cherokee protested, seventy-nine of them signed a treaty agreeing to move. The United States Senate passed that treaty by just one vote. The Cherokee had to leave.

Many were arrested and moved by river to the new territory. Those left behind, about 18,000 men, women, and children, were forced to travel overland. The journey turned to tragedy as the cold, hungry Cherokee people marched westward, leaving 4,000 dead "on the trail where they cried." The route they took was later named "The Trail of Tears."

Twelve-year-old Wilma was a descendant of some of those long-ago Cherokee who had walked "The Trail of Tears." She remembered that sad story of her people when, in 1957, she and her family were "relocated." This time the United States government decided to move some American Indians who lived in the country into the cities. The government believed that the move would give the Indians an opportunity to learn new job skills they couldn't acquire otherwise. It was hoped that these new skills would help Indians get better jobs for better pay.

So, just as their ancestors had, the Mankillers were forced to start all over again in a strange new place. They found themselves in San Francisco, California in a poor, crime-ridden neighborhood. But Wilma's father refused to believe that, just because his family had moved away from all that was familiar, they had to leave behind their Cherokee tribal culture as well. He learned the new job skills that the government expected of him, but he also kept intact his family's proud heritage. This was not an easy task for Wilma's father, but he succeeded.

So Wilma Mankiller grew up in an atmosphere of reading and discussion and learning which, she said later, set the framework for her life.

When she was older, Wilma married a businessman from South America during the 1960s and had two daughters, Felicia and Gina. In 1969 Wilma decided to go back to school to learn more about sociology and community development.

While she was at San Francisco State University, some members of an organization called the American Indian Movement (AIM) seized an old prison on the island of Alcatraz off the coast of California. They did it to protest the United States government's treatment of Native Americans. They attracted national attention.

53

Suddenly it seemed that everyone in America was talking about Indians.

Wilma was no exception. In fact, that rebellion at Alcatraz gave her ideas that changed the course of her life. She started to volunteer among San Francisco's Indian population. She studied tribal governments and Cherokee history. The information she uncovered about broken treaties and promises, disappointments and despair, made her angry—and determined to make a difference. Wilma Mankiller had become an activist.

In 1975 the United States finally passed a law giving Cherokees "self-determination." This meant the Cherokee had the right to look after their own affairs and to live with less influence from the U.S. government.

Wilma could see that the tribe's need for jobs, education, health care, and housing was enormous. So after divorcing her husband in 1977, Wilma returned to Oklahoma with her children. Remembering her own happiness as a little girl in Oklahoma, she wanted her girls to enjoy life in the Oklahoma countryside as she had.

Once they got to Oklahoma, Wilma worked hard for her people. She knew that her people had much to do and to learn before they could be truly self-sufficient. But Wilma remembered her tribe's history.

No tribe had ever learned the white man's ways faster than the Cherokee. As early as 1809, just a dozen years after the death of George Washington, the Cherokee had formed a National Council. They drew up a constitution. They built schools and roads and settled on farms and ranches. Each town had its own chief and its own council. The National Council elected a principal chief. Their constitution called for a general election every four years to name a principal chief and a deputy chief who were similar to a president and vice president.

If her ancestors were self-sufficient, Wilma reasoned, then surely the Cherokee could succeed again in looking after themselves.

Wilma helped to get government grants to pay for some of the services they needed. She set up housing projects, programs for the elderly, nursery schools, and a gardening business. Again and again, Wilma spoke out to encourage self-sufficiency among the 120,000 members of the Cherokee tribe.

Another life-changing event in Wilma's life occurred one fall day in 1979 when Wilma had a bad automobile accident. She was in the hospital for many months. Her face was crushed, her ribs and her legs were badly broken. She needed plastic surgery to restore her face and had a series of operations to repair her shattered bones.

Wilma had plenty of time to think about more ways to help her people while she was in the hospital. In a little over a year she was back at work and had convinced the government to grant money to some rural Cherokees to build a twenty-six-mile-long waterline for themselves.

The male leaders of the Cherokee tribe began to notice Wilma. In 1983 she was asked to run for election as deputy chief. And when Chief Ross Swimmer went to Washington, D.C. to take over as the head of the Bureau of Indian Affairs, Wilma Mankiller took over the duties of principal chief of the Cherokee Nation. Then, in 1987, Wilma ran for a full four-year term. She won the election and became the very first woman in history to be *elected* as Cherokee chief.

Wilma's days as chief were always crammed with activity. She had frequent meetings in the Cherokee capital of Tahlequah in the "green country" of northeast Oklahoma. Often she had to fly to the state capital in Oklahoma City, and she was becoming well known in Washington, D.C., too, talking to members of Congress about all the things the Cherokee needed. Wilma's second husband, a full-blood Cherokee named Charlie Soap, worked with her to develop more community programs to help the Cherokee live productive, self-sufficient lives.

In 1991 it was time for another election. Although Wilma's broken bones had long since healed, and the scars of plastic surgery were barely noticeable, Wilma had developed a disease of the nervous system and she'd had a kidney transplant. Although her health wasn't perfect, she felt that there was still a great deal of work left for her to do. There were quite a few programs in place that Wilma wanted to see all the way through to completion. She and Charlie talked it over and Wilma decided to run for a second full term as principal chief.

On June 15, 1991, Wilma Mankiller was once again elected to serve for four more years, winning that election with 83 percent of the vote.

The Cherokee Nation moved toward the twenty-first century with Wilma leading the way in Tahlequah. As she began her second term, Wilma was certain that her people could thrive and prosper in the modern world without ever losing sight of Cherokee customs, language, ceremonies, and tribal culture. Her Cherokee elders had taught her well about looking ahead. "Turn what has been done into a better path," they said. "If you're a leader, think about the impact of your decisions on seven generations into the future."

Wilma looked forward to beginning a national program for all American Indians, not just the Cherokee. She proposed to work with other American Indian leaders to bring all of America's great Indian tribes to greater self-reliance, while preserving for future generations the enriching values, languages, and traditions that have been passed down through the centuries.

Golda Meir

ISRAELI HERO

"The last thing Israelis want is to win wars. We want peace."

—Golda Meir

Eight-year-old Golda Mabovitch hid behind her mother's skirt when the tall, slim, handsome man approached. "Don't be afraid," said her mother. "It's your Papa."

Golda barely remembered him. Three years had passed since 1903 when Moshe Mabovitch had left his wife and three daughters in Russia and set out for America to seek a better life for his family. Now at last, Golda, her two sisters, and her mother and father were together in Milwaukee, Wisconsin.

At first the five of them were crowded into one room. It was not the America Golda had always pictured. But at least there were no Cossacks riding through the streets with their swords and whips crying, "Death to the Jews!"

Before long the Mabovitch family moved. Golda's mother, Bluma, borrowed some money and made a down payment on a grocery store with an apartment attached. The five small rooms seemed huge to Golda and her sisters Shana and Tzipka. Golda's father worked as a carpenter, and her older sister Shana found a job in a factory. Tzipka was too little to be of much help, so Golda was the one who cleaned the shop in the morning while Bluma went out to the wholesale markets.

One of things Golda loved about America was the fact that girls as well as boys were sent to school, and school was free. Back in Russia, Golda had been discouraged from going to school.

One day, when Golda was fifteen, a regular customer at the store announced that he had fallen in love with Golda. He asked permission to marry her. Golda's mother agreed, and informed Golda that she'd be getting married soon. Arranged marriages were quite ordinary back in Russia, and Bluma thought she'd found a good husband for her daughter!

Tearfully, Golda wrote a letter to her sister Shana, who was married now and living in Denver. Shana understood exactly how Golda felt. Her parents had once wanted her to marry a man she didn't love too. Shana and her husband, Shamai, invited Golda to come to Denver to go to school.

A few weeks later, Golda lowered her suitcase out the window, ate her breakfast, and said a pleasant goodbye to her parents. But instead of going to school, she went to the railway station. Golda ran away from home.

Several times a week a group of young people gathered at Shana and Shamai's apartment for tea and conversation. Golda was fascinated as she listened to debates and discussions. One young man Golda found especially interesting was Morris Myerson. He was only one of several bachelors who asked the pretty, auburn-haired Golda for dates.

Golda grew more and more interested in a political movement called *Zionism*. Zionists believed that Jews, who had been driven from one country to another for hundreds of years, needed to have a place to live where they didn't have to be afraid—a land where Jews could be free to govern themselves. Golda believed this land should be Palestine, where Jews had lived longer than any other people. She joined an organization that raised money to buy land in Palestine—mostly rocky hillsides or mosquito-infested marshes—which was all they were able to buy.

When World War I broke out, millions of Jews became homeless. More and more Golda thought about Palestine. She decided that as soon as she could, she was going to go there and devote her life to creating a Jewish homeland. She told Morris of her intentions. But Morris was not interested in a homeland for Jews in Palestine, or any other place

To Golda, the idea of personally helping to rebuild the ancient homeland of the Jews seemed the most important thing she could do with her life. She planned to go there to live on a *kibbutz*—a kind of commune where everyone shares in all of the work. If Morris could not understand she would have to go alone.

Morris decided that despite his misgivings about going to Palestine, he loved Golda and couldn't live without her. They were married in December 1917.

In May 1921 after the war ended, Golda and Morris traveled to Palestine. They settled in the new Jewish city of Tel Aviv. Golda found that kibbutz life suited her perfectly, but Morris didn't like it at all. They reached a compromise. They agreed to move from the kibbutz to live in the old city of Jerusalem. Golda would be a housewife and they would have children.

Menachem Myerson was born in November 1924.

Morris was delighted. This was the way he wanted things to be. He worked as a bookkeeper while Golda tended their small apartment and cared for the baby. Golda tried to be content. But one spring evening she began to cry. She couldn't seem to stop the tears. She wanted to go back to work with the people who were trying to create a Jewish homeland. Morris said, "Go if you must. If you want to come back, I'll be waiting."

She took the baby and went to the kibbutz. But she missed Morris. Six months later she returned to Jerusalem, to the life Morris wanted her to live. The following year blond, blue-eyed baby Sarah was born. Golda took in washing to help with expenses. She had to wash the clothes by hand in a bathtub, sloshing them on a rough washboard. But even as busy as she was, Golda found time to volunteer at the Labor Council offices. Sometimes she brought the children along with her so that she could stay involved with the work she loved.

One day, when Golda was thirty-one, she was called to the Labor Council office and was offered the job of secretary of the Women's Labor Council. She accepted, and her work became more exciting and rewarding than ever. When she was thirty-seven, Golda was elected to the Executive Committee. She was now truly one of the most important people in Palestine.

Golda's children adjusted well to their new life. They liked their Hebrew school and enjoyed their music lessons. But while Menachem and Sarah were learning to play the cello and the violin, Jewish children in Hitler's Germany weren't so lucky. They lived in a place where shops refused to sell to Jews, where Jewish children were not allowed to go to the same schools as other kids, and where thousands of people were arrested—just for being Jewish.

Golda wanted to bring the German Jews to Palestine where they would be safe. She tried in every way she knew to have Palestine declared an official Jewish state. It was obvious that a war with Germany was coming. Then there would be no escape for Jews trapped in the countries Hitler dominated.

World War II began in Europe in 1939. Throughout the war, Golda struggled to try to get as many Jews to safety as possible. But by the time the war had ended in 1945, *six million* Jews had been murdered. Golda announced, "Those . . . were the last Jews to die without defending themselves." She knew that her people must have their own state, where their own laws and army could protect them.

Jewish leader David Ben-Gurion told the British, who controlled Palestine at that time, that they must get out and allow the Jews to have their own state. The British refused. A revolt began. Bridges were destroyed. Guns stolen. Boatloads of refugees from Europe dared to try to sneak past the British warships that guarded the coast to keep them out. The Jews of Palestine refused to give up the dream of having their own homeland. Even 100,000 British soldiers stationed there could not keep order. They'd had enough. The British referred the whole problem of Palestine to the United Nations.

The United Nations delegates debated the problem and announced their decision. Palestine would be divided into *two* independent nations—one Arab and the other Jewish. In six months, a Jewish country would finally become a reality. It would be called Israel.

But the Arab nations didn't agree. They were ready

to go to war with the tiny new nation. David Ben-Gurion called an emergency meeting that Golda attended. "We need $25 million dollars to equip the army. It is unlikely that we can expect to get it from America."

Golda jumped to her feet. "Let me go to America. Maybe I can get the money."

She arrived in New York and spoke to the United Council of Jewish Federations. Before the afternoon was over the people who heard her had pledged more than $25 million dollars!

Golda made speeches in almost every state. Money poured in. Weapons and ammunition and tanks were bought. When Golda returned to Israel, David Ben-Gurion said, "Someday when our history is written it will be said that there was a Jewish woman who got the money which made the nation possible."

There was a war with neighboring Arab countries, but the Jews fought valiantly. In February 1949, the United Nations helped to negotiate a truce, and the country was finally at peace. Prime Minister Ben-Gurion appointed Golda as Israel's first Minister of Labor. She held that position for seven years. Then Ben-Gurion asked her to take another job. She became Foreign Minister of Israel. It was the second-highest job in the land. Ben-Gurion asked her to take a Hebrew name too. She chose one as close to Myerson as possible—Meir—which means "illuminate" in Hebrew.

In 1966 Golda announced her retirement. She'd served in every Israeli Cabinet since the first election in 1949, and she thought that at last she'd be able to take it easy and have time to play with her grandchildren. But in 1969 the prime minister, Levi Eshkol, died suddenly. Israel needed a new prime minister and chose Golda.

She was nearly seventy, but once again, she answered her country's call.

The young Jewish nation was bordered by countries at odds with its policies. The Israelis tried always to be alert. They never knew when they might have to fight. But on October 6, 1973, they were taken by surprise when Egypt and Syria suddenly attacked. After a three-week struggle, Israeli forces managed to defend their country successfully, but 2,500 Israeli soldiers died. Some citizens blamed their leaders, including Golda, for being unprepared. She agreed with them and retired in 1974. A new government came to power.

In 1978 Golda Meir died of leukemia. She was eighty years old. People all over the world were saddened by the loss of this brave, wise, kind person—the first woman Prime Minister of Israel.

Sandra Day O'Connor

FIRST WOMAN SUPREME COURT JUSTICE

"The individual can make things happen."

—Sandra Day O'Connor

When Harry Day proposed to Ada Mae Wilkey, she said "yes" right away. Marrying Harry meant that Ada would be giving up the fun and excitement of living in El Paso, Texas for Harry's far-away Arizona ranch, the Lazy B. She'd be setting up housekeeping in a tiny four-room house. There'd be no running water, no electricity—not even an indoor bathroom, and the place was twenty miles away from the nearest town. But Ada Mae was in love, and she knew that the Lazy B meant the world to Harry.

Ada Mae never regretted her decision to marry Harry. And three years later, in 1930, they had their first child, Sandra. Little Sandra didn't mind one bit that her ranch home was isolated. Ada Mae always had time to read to her from the *Book of Knowledge* or *National Geographic* as Sandra looked at colorful pictures of far-away places and people. Before long, Sandra could read all by herself.

When Sandra was five, Ada Mae and Harry decided that it was time for her to go to a regular school. But there were no schools near the Lazy B. They sent

Sandra to live with her lively Grandmother Wilkey in El Paso to attend the Radford Girl's School.

Everyone at Radford was warm and friendly, but still, Sandra felt homesick for the Lazy B. Every vacation she'd bring home some of her new friends to meet Harry and Ada Mae and to ride horses and play games. Sometimes they had so much fun that when it was time to go back to the city they'd hide in the haystack, hoping to miss the train.

When Sandra was eight years old, her little sister Ann was born. Her brother Alan was born two years later. Sandra attended Radford through the seventh grade, then insisted that she wanted to return to the ranch for the eighth grade so she'd have time with her little brother and sister. Her parents agreed and dropped Sandra off at a neighboring ranch every morning where the school bus would pick her up. Then came a long, uncomfortable ride over bumpy roads. It was dark when Sandra left home in the mornings and dark when she got home at night.

But Sandra wanted to play with her brother and sister on the weekends, so she maintained that difficult schedule for a whole school year. But when it was time for high school the following year she agreed to go back to Grandmother Wilkey's.

When Sandra enrolled in Austin High School, she was tall, tanned, and graceful. The tomboy had turned into an elegant teenager. Sandra had developed quite a talent for drama too. She had what her teachers called "stage presence"—the ability to appear calm and in charge of a situation even when she was nervous inside. She had a natural ability to organize her thoughts and to present them quickly and logically.

When she was only sixteen, Sandra completed every

requirement for a high school diploma! She prepared for her early graduation and dreamed of going to college. She wanted very much to attend Stanford University. Sandra knew that there would be tough competition for admission to the university. It was 1949 and many thousands of soldiers returning from World War II were heading back to college too. Even if she could get admitted, attending Stanford was expensive. But the Day family believed in Sandra. "If you want to go to Stanford, and you can get in," Harry promised, "we'll figure out how to pay for it."

The university staff was impressed with Sandra's outstanding academic record and her long list of extracurricular activities. They accepted her application. Sandra wasn't surprised. "I knew I'd be admitted to Stanford," she told her friends. "I was so sure that I never even applied to any other college!"

Sandra decided to study economics to develop her business skills. She worked hard as usual, and her grades made her parents proud. But Sandra didn't just study all the time. She loved going to the movies with her friends. She enjoyed dancing too, and sometimes on weekends she went skiing. Sandra Day was thoroughly enjoying college life!

Sandra signed up for a course in business law and found it fascinating. She loved figuring out how to come up with fair solutions to complicated problems. She became interested in the study of law.

Luckily for Sandra, the university had just started a new program which allowed fourth-year students to add first-year law courses to their class schedules. A family friend tried to prepare her for disappointment. "Don't be too disappointed if you can't get into the program," he warned. "Not many law students are women, you know. They may not want you."

Sandra didn't give up hope, and that fall she was one of only seven women admitted to Stanford's freshman law class. She took courses in criminal and civil law and learned how to draw up legal contracts. "I loved my classes," she said. "I thoroughly enjoyed law school." Sandra was also selected to be an editor of the *Stanford Law Review* when she was just a second-year student.

Sandra was in the library one evening, working on an article for the *Review,* when she first met John Jay O'Connor III. John was a year behind her in school, but they had both been asked to work on the same article. Checking facts for a law article could have been boring, but the two young people found that they were actually having a good time. They studied together almost every night after that, and before long they decided to get married. Sandra invited John to the Lazy B Ranch to meet her family. Everyone agreed that John would make a fine husband for Sandra.

Sandra graduated in June 1952, *magna cum laude.* Those Latin words mean "with great distinction." Sandra had the third-highest marks in her class. A young man named William Rehnquist came in first.

Sandra started searching for a job. She rode the cable cars up and down the hills of San Francisco, going from one law firm to another, telling them about her qualifications and asking for work.

"We've never hired a woman before," was what most of them said. Some even added, "and we don't intend to do it now."

"You could work here as our secretary," offered one firm.

"No thanks," said Sandra.

Sandra had plans and dreams for her life. She was a qualified lawyer, and she wanted the job which would give her the opportunity to prove it.

Finally Sandra was hired as deputy for the District Attorney of San Mateo County. She'd be working near Stanford, where John still had a year of school to complete.

On December 20, 1952, Sandra and John were married at the Lazy B Ranch. The next year Sandra was promoted. Her new title was Deputy County Attorney.

After John's graduation from Stanford in 1953, he was drafted into the United States Army and sent to Frankfurt, Germany, where he gave legal advice to military courts. Sandra loved her job, but she didn't want to be separated from John. Sandra became a lawyer for the United States Armed Forces, and she and John stayed in Germany for three years.

In 1957, Sandra and John were expecting their first baby. It was time to go home to America. Little Scott O'Connor was born in Arizona. Later, Sandra and John had two more boys, Brian and Jay.

Sandra stayed busy. Although she wasn't actively practicing law, she volunteered for a number of organizations. Sandra was very good at getting things done. Her hard work inspired other people to do their best. Every committee or organization Sandra joined noticed improvements because of her efforts.

After Sandra's youngest boy started preschool in 1965, she started her legal career again in the Arizona attorney general's office. There Sandra learned just how state government works. She worked on cases for the health department, the welfare department, and the treasurer's office. She soon became an expert on state government matters, and her opinions were often quoted in the newspapers. Once Sandra knew what the problems were, she was able to find solutions.

In 1972 Sandra became a Republican state senator in Arizona which allowed her to help write new laws and to change old laws that she thought were unfair. She helped strike down a law that said women couldn't work more than eight hours a day while men could work as much as they wanted. She also changed a law that said that a husband could control property which really belonged to his wife.

People realized that Sandra was honest, fair, and hard working. After her first term was up, she ran for the state senate twice and won both times. She probably could have become a famous politician if she'd wanted to. But she felt that with her talents she would make a good judge. Sandra ran for the office and was elected as a judge for Arizona's Maricopa County Superior Court.

People all over Arizona said, "Sandra Day O'Connor is really fair." Even if they didn't like what she decided, they had to admit that Judge O'Connor always did exactly what the law said. When a jury found somebody guilty of a crime, it was her job to decide how that person would be punished. Some people had to pay fines, others had to go to jail. Sometimes she even had to sentence a criminal to death. She hated that part, but she always followed what the law said she must do.

The governor of Arizona then was Bruce Babbit. One day he called Sandra. "How would you like to be a judge on the Arizona Court of Appeals?" he asked.

Sandra realized that this was a great honor and a really important job. She talked it over with John, and he encouraged her to accept the governor's offer. She did, and held that job until 1981 when President Ronald Reagan chose her for another even more important one.

President Reagan nominated Sandra Day O'Connor to be the first woman in history to serve on the United States Supreme Court—the highest court in America. The Supreme Court helps lower courts interpret laws. Supreme Court justices keep their jobs for life. Sandra already knew one of the justices. He was her old Stanford classmate, William Rehnquist!

The Supreme Court has rules about where each justice sits. The Chief Justice always sits in the middle. The newest justice always sits at the far right, so that was where Sandra sat when she was first appointed. When the next justice was appointed, Sandra moved to the seat on the far left. When yet another justice was appointed, she moved to the second seat on the right. Perhaps someday she will sit in the middle and be the Chief Justice. But wherever she sits, she will always have the distinction of being the first woman ever appointed to the United States Supreme Court.

Eleanor Roosevelt

"Given the world situation, there is no such thing as being a bystander."

—Eleanor Roosevelt

In October 1884, in New York City, a popular and wealthy young couple welcomed their first child—a little girl. Anna and Elliot Roosevelt named their daughter Anna Eleanor, but everyone called her by her middle name, Eleanor.

Eleanor's father Elliot was a handsome, fun-loving man who enjoyed hunting, horseback riding, and yachting with his friends. Once he even went to India to hunt tigers with his older brother Theodore, who later became the twenty-sixth president of the United States. Her mother, Anna Hall Roosevelt, liked to wear pretty clothes and go to parties where her striking good looks always made her the center of attention. Eleanor felt that her father was perfect even though his drinking sometimes made him moody and hard to get along with. She felt that her mother was surely the most beautiful person she had ever seen. And when her two little brothers, Elliot Jr. and Hall, were born, she thought that they were the cutest babies in the world. But shy, quiet Eleanor only thought of herself as awkward and homely.

When Eleanor was just nine years old her mother died, and she and her brothers were sent to live with their Grandmother Hall. Her father was only allowed to visit the children once in a while, and Eleanor grew more and more lonely. Then, the very next spring, her little brother Elliot died from scarlet fever. After that, the visits from Eleanor's father were even fewer than before. His drinking became worse, and in 1894, he fell to his death from an upstairs window in his home. At the age of ten, Eleanor was an orphan.

Grandmother Hall thought that poetry, history, and French, along with dancing lessons, were all the education necessary for a young woman, so those were the things Eleanor was allowed to learn. Eleanor went to school and to dancing classes wearing clothes that had belonged to her mother and to her aunts when they were girls.

Grandmother Hall had no idea that styles had changed. Poor Eleanor! While her classmates wore fashionable long skirts swirling around their ankles, Eleanor was miserable in out-of-date dresses that barely covered her knees.

When she was fourteen, Uncle Teddy Roosevelt invited Eleanor to a Christmas dance at his house. As usual, her dress was out of style. She felt ugly and uncomfortable. She was happily surprised when a distant cousin, tall, handsome, sixteen-year-old Franklin Roosevelt, asked her to dance.

The next year, Eleanor was sent to a school for girls in England, and from the moment she arrived at Allenswood School, she loved being there. Although her education in New York hadn't prepared her very well, she soon caught up with the other students. Before long she was one of the smartest and best-liked girls at the school. And she bought some fashionable new clothes to wear too!

After three happy years at Allenswood, Eleanor was called home by Grandmother Hall. Eleanor was nearly eighteen, and it was time for her to be introduced to society. This meant lots of fancy-dress parties and balls. Eleanor still hated parties, but at least now she had pretty clothes to wear.

It was considered proper in those days for wealthy women to be involved in charity work, and Eleanor really enjoyed working with poor immigrant children. She taught them dancing and gymnastics and helped them with their English.

Another reason Eleanor enjoyed being back in New York was her cousin Franklin. He seemed to be attracted to her shy charm and quick mind. He made her feel pretty. When she was nineteen and Franklin was twenty-one, he asked her to marry him. She accepted happily

Eleanor and Franklin Roosevelt were married on St. Patrick's Day in 1905. By then Eleanor's Uncle Teddy was President of the United States, and because Eleanor's own father was dead, Uncle Teddy gave the bride away. This was one time that Eleanor didn't mind wearing someone else's old clothes. In her Grandmother Hall's high-necked satin and lace wedding dress, Eleanor looked lovely. Some guests even remarked that she looked like her beautiful mother.

Sometimes Eleanor and Franklin visited Uncle Teddy in the White House. The President often suggested that Franklin should get into politics. "My boy," he would say, "there is no higher calling than the public service where you work for the betterment of the lives of your fellow men."

Uncle Teddy assumed that if Franklin ever ran for office, he'd be a Republican, but in 1910 Franklin decided to run for the New York State Senate as a Democrat—and he won.

At that time United States senators weren't elected directly. The legislatures for each state decided who would represent the state in Washington, D.C. The New York Legislature chose Franklin. Then in 1913, he was appointed Assistant Secretary of the Navy by President Woodrow Wilson, and the Roosevelts moved to Washington, D.C.

In 1914 World War I broke out in Europe. The United States joined the war in 1917. Franklin's job was to build up the Navy. Eleanor hated war, but she worked hard for the Red Cross, making sandwiches and coffee for soldiers passing through Washington. She visited naval hospitals and knitted sweaters and socks for Navy men all through the war years.

By this time the Roosevelts had five children, and in the summer the whole family enjoyed vacations on a small island between Canada and Maine called Campobello. They were there in August of 1921 when Franklin suddenly became ill. He had caught polio. In those days there was no vaccine to prevent the terrible disease and no medicine to cure it. Soon Franklin could no longer walk or even move his legs.

Franklin's mother wanted him to go home to New York and live as an invalid for the rest of his life. "That's the last thing he should do," said Eleanor, "and I won't let him."

Franklin tried hard to regain the use of his legs. He did every exercise the doctors gave him. Yet, two years passed before he could even wiggle his big toe.

Franklin's friends wanted him to stay interested in politics even if he couldn't walk. One of his closest advisors had the idea that if Eleanor became involved in politics, perhaps Franklin would be jealous and get interested in the Democratic party again.

Eleanor wasn't so sure, but she wanted to help Franklin, so she took the suggestion. She joined the Women's Trade Union League and the Women's Division of the Democratic State Committee. Before long she was making speeches and even editing the Women's Division newspaper. The idea worked! Franklin began meeting with political leaders and talking about elections. By 1928 Franklin was able to walk with metal braces on his legs if someone helped him a little, and he became an important person in the Democratic party once again. And Eleanor had become the best-known woman in the whole state of New York!

In 1928, Franklin ran for the office of governor of New York and won. He won again in 1932. Then in 1932, Franklin was nominated by the Democratic Party as its candidate for President of the United States. He won again. At the age of forty-eight, Eleanor Roosevelt moved into the White House—the very same grand house where she'd visited her Uncle Teddy so many years before.

No president's wife in history had ever held press conferences, but Eleanor did. She knew that half the people in America were women and that they were interested in what she had to say. Every Thursday morning she met with newspaperwomen from all over the country. She had a regular monthly question-and-answer column in a magazine and also a weekly newspaper column about life in the White House. In her own gentle way she made the president's activities interesting to just about every American.

It seemed that the busier Eleanor's life got, the more she found to do. "I think I must have a good deal of my uncle Teddy Roosevelt in me," she said, "because I love a good fight and I could not, at any age, really be contented to take my place in a warm corner by the fireside and simply look on."

Once she went on a tour of a very poor neighborhood near the Capitol Building. She visited a public home for the aged too. She was so shocked by the terrible living conditions she found that she went to Congress and demanded that they do something to make life better for the people who lived in those neighborhoods. "We should be ashamed," she said. "I was sickened. If that is the way we care for people who are not able to care for themselves, we are at a pretty low ebb of civilization." Congress did as she asked.

Mail poured into the White House for Eleanor—300,000 letters during the first nine months alone! Franklin needed Eleanor to go out into the country for him to places he couldn't go. She went down West Virginia mine shafts to see how the miners worked. She visited shacks covered in coal dust where miners' families lived. Back in Washington, she proposed a model housing project, along with clinics and schools, for the miners. Franklin saw that everything was done as she wished.

Eleanor made many other trips for Franklin. She went to Puerto Rico and the Virgin Islands. She visited the Dust Bowl in the midwestern United States. "My eyes," Franklin proudly called her.

With the help of government officials, Eleanor started the National Youth Administration. This agency arranged part-time work for high school and college boys and girls who needed to work in order to continue their educations.

Eleanor Roosevelt was extremely interested in the welfare of black people. In hundreds of speeches she insisted that black people must have equal opportunities for education and jobs, and that they must not be treated as inferior Americans. She helped many black people to find jobs in government and in private industry. She raised money to build and improve schools and hospitals in black communities.

It hadn't taken Eleanor very long to become the most active First Lady in American history. In 1936, Franklin was re-elected and Eleanor expanded her lectures, her investigations, and her writing. By 1939 people all around the world were worried about what was happening in Germany. Adolf Hitler, Germany's dictator, was trying to conquer the whole world. Eleanor felt that the United States should oppose aggression and slavery. She spoke against Hitler and his goals. Sometimes she was booed for what she said, but she never backed down. Gradually people started to agree with her.

After Hitler invaded Poland, Franklin convinced Congress to let the United States help countries that Hitler was attacking. By 1940, Hitler's armies had overrun five more countries. Franklin decided that he'd better run for a third term as president. No one had ever tried it before. But once again, he won. The United States entered World War II when the Japanese, who were Germany's allies, attacked Pearl Harbor on December 7, 1941. Then Germany and Italy declared war on America too.

People were worried—and frightened. Eleanor made speeches to calm their fears. After becoming the Assistant Head of the Office of Civil Defense, Eleanor visited factories producing war supplies to encourage people to work as hard as they could for their country. She visited military hospitals. She even went overseas and visited army camps and shipyards, stopping to talk to as many soldiers as she could.

She made a trip to the South Pacific in 1943. It was a hard journey for Eleanor. She was nearly sixty years old. She lost 30 pounds and caught pneumonia. Yet she didn't even rest when she got back to Washington. She began calling the families of soldiers she had seen.

In 1944, even though Franklin was tired and ill, he told Eleanor that he would run for a fourth term. He wanted to finish the wartime job he had taken on and form an organization called the United Nations just as soon as the war ended.

Eleanor was worried about Franklin's health. After he won the election, he grew weaker each day. The opening meeting to establish the United Nations was planned for April 25, 1945. Franklin decided to go away for a short rest and asked Eleanor to stay at the White House and attend to a few things for him. But on April 12 the president's secretary called Eleanor. "The president has died," he told her.

Eleanor thought that after Franklin's death she'd live a quiet life at her old home in New York. She was mistaken. The new president, Harry S. Truman, asked Eleanor to serve as America's delegate to the brand new United Nations Organization, where she helped pass the statement known as the Declaration of Human Rights.

During the 1950s, Eleanor continued to travel and meet with world leaders. She remained very active within the Democratic party. When John F. Kennedy was elected president, she became his friend and advisor. But in 1962

Eleanor became too sick to continue her activities. Her children brought her home to her house in New York City. They were all with her when she died on November 7, 1962.

One of Eleanor's friends, American politician Adlai Stevenson, stated, "She walked in the slums and ghettos of the world, not on a tour of inspection . . . but as one who could not feel contentment when others were hungry."

Margaret Thatcher

THE IRON LADY

"If you have a sense of purpose and a sense of direction, I believe people will follow you."

—Margaret Thatcher

Grantham, England, 120 miles north of London, is a tidy, comfortable town, not too big and not too small. Margaret Hilda Roberts was born there in 1926, and she and her sister Muriel grew up in an apartment upstairs from their father Alfred's grocery store. Their home, like Grantham, was tidy and comfortable, not too big and not too small. Alfred Robert's store also served as the neighborhood post office, and when Margaret and Muriel were teenagers they both helped out, waiting on customers and keeping the shelves freshly stocked and the goods neatly displayed.

The girls' parents took a great deal of interest in their education. Alfred Roberts hadn't been able to finish school himself, but he'd taught himself by using the library. He was determined that his daughters, especially Margaret, who appeared eager to learn, would have the kind of education he'd missed. When Muriel and Margaret were little girls they didn't go to the elementary school closest to the shop. Instead, they walked to a school at the other end of town, where Alfred thought the teaching was better and where the girls could meet children from Grantham's most successful families.

When it was time for them to go to high school, the two were sent to Kesteven & Grantham Girls School. Parents were charged a fee to send their children to Kesteven, but Margaret studied extra-hard and won a scholarship, so her parents only had to pay for her sister's tuition. Although the Roberts family wasn't poor, Alfred Roberts was always thrifty and tried to save money wherever he could.

The Roberts family was very interested in Grantham politics. Alfred Roberts was a member of the town council for twenty-five years, and once even served a term as mayor. So it was no wonder that Margaret was interested in politics too. Kesteven had a debating club where students took opposing sides to questions on current events. Margaret Roberts was hard to beat. Her arguments were always well-prepared and she spoke with self-confidence. She even took elocution lessons to improve the way she spoke. Margaret played field hockey very well too. In fact, she became the youngest captain the school had ever had.

Margaret worked hard at school and did well enough in her high school studies to be accepted at one of the world's most famous universities—Oxford. But there was one problem. Latin was a required subject at Oxford and Kesteven hadn't offered the language. Albert Roberts hired a tutor, and Margaret passed the entrance examinations.

Even though Margaret was really interested in politics, she knew that there wasn't much money to be made in it. She realized that she was going to have to earn a living. Chemistry seemed to offer lots of career opportunities, so she devoted her university years to scientific subjects. Unfortunately, Margaret was never able to use her excellent debating talent while she was at Oxford. (It wasn't until 1963 that the Oxford debating forum admitted women as members!)

Margaret realized before she'd completed her studies that perhaps she would have been happier had she studied law instead of chemistry. Still, she graduated in 1947 with a chemistry degree and was hired immediately as a research chemist for a plastics manufacturer. But because Margaret had never given up her interest in politics, she often attended political meetings in her free time.

In the United Kingdom the part of the government responsible for making laws is called *Parliament*. Parliament is divided into two "houses." One is the *House of Lords* and the other is the *House of Commons*. There are thousands of members in the House of Lords. They are people with inherited titles—like Lords and Ladies, Barons and Baronesses—and others like bishops, judges, and politicians who have been given titles by a King or Queen. The House of Commons is made up of 635 men and women who have been elected by the people. There are two major political parties in Parliament, the Conservative Party and the Labor Party.

In 1950 Margaret Roberts was selected by the local Conservative party to run for a seat in the House of Commons. At 23 she was the youngest woman candidate in Great Britain. She knew that she wouldn't win because people in the district were strong Labor Party supporters. Margaret knew she'd be running mainly to gain political experience. But she worked very hard on her election campaign anyway. She worked every day at the plastics factory, then spent all of her free time campaigning. She impressed people by the way she spoke and by the many hours she spent campaigning. But Margaret lost the election, as she had expected.

In 1951 Margaret took a new job with an ice cream manufacturer. This new position allowed her to spend more time on her political interests. She tried again for a seat in Parliament. She lost once more, but by fewer votes this time.

It was while she was campaigning in 1950 that Margaret met Denis Thatcher. Denis was ten years older than she was, a successful businessman who was also a member of the Conservative party. They were married in 1951, and two years later Margaret had twins, Carol and Mark. After her marriage to Denis, Margaret finally had time to study law, and when the twins were just four months old, Margaret Thatcher became a lawyer.

During the next few years, Margaret devoted her time to raising her children and practicing law. Then, in 1959, she had another chance to run for a seat in the House of Commons in a strongly Conservative neighborhood. She won easily, and at the age of 32 at last began the political career she had always wanted.

Margaret was a newcomer and not well-known to her fellow lawmakers. But she was soon noticed when she introduced her first bill, a carefully worded idea for a law that she thought was important. The bill was similar to what is called in the United States the "sunshine laws." These laws prevent government councils and committees from meeting in secret. She had learned that some of the councils controlled by the Labor Party didn't allow the public, or even newspaper reporters, to attend their meetings. Margaret Thatcher thought this was unfair, and she wanted a law to prevent this from happening. On June 1, 1961, her bill became law.

She quickly became well-known to Conservative Party leaders. In 1962 she was appointed a "junior minister." This wasn't as important as "minister," but it was a good step forward in her political career.

In Great Britain, whichever party wins the most seats in the House of Commons is declared the winner of the national election. Sometimes the Labor Party wins and sometimes the Conservative party does. The winning party forms the government. Even when the Conservative Party wasn't the winner, Margaret Thatcher continued to be one of the best-known speakers in the house. When the Conservative Party was in power, though, Margaret's positions grew even more important. In 1970 she was named Minister of Education and Science. She believed that each neighborhood should be able to decide what kinds of programs it wanted its schools to have. She thought that parents and teachers should help make important decisions about their schools and that it should not all be left up to government to decide.

An election to decide who would lead the Conservative Party was scheduled for 1975, and the leading candidate was Sir Keith Joseph. But during the campaign he made some remarks which were insulting to some of Great Britain's minorities, and Margaret Thatcher became Joseph's replacement. Most people in England were willing to bet that a woman couldn't get elected. But by the time the votes were counted, Margaret Thatcher, at 49, became the first woman in 700 years of Parliament's history to lead an important political party.

Margaret felt strong that her party could do a better

job of governing England than the Labor party, and she made many speeches all over the country telling people what she thought. When it was time for another general election in 1979 she knew that the people had listened. The Conservatives won. Margaret Thatcher, as leader of her party, became the first woman prime minister of Great Britain.

Times were difficult in Britain. Businesses had failed and many people had lost their jobs. Still, Margaret believed that her ideas of cutting government spending and taxing people less would work. She refused to change her views even when it seemed that most people thought she was wrong. She began to be known the world over. Her hatred for communism was so strong that the leaders of the Soviet Union, a communist country, called her "The Iron Lady." They meant it as an insult, but Margaret didn't mind the name at all. Slowly things began to improve in Great Britain. More people got jobs and the future looked a little better.

Suddenly in April 1982, Argentina invaded a group of islands known as the Falklands, off the east coast of South America. Those islands belonged to Great Britain, and the people who lived there were loyal to the British government. Margaret decided to send forty ships steaming toward Argentina. Aboard the ships were 2,000 soldiers and sailors. "We have to recover those islands," Margaret said. And the British people agreed.

Still, Argentina would not give up the Falkland Islands. More ships and troops were sent. Ten weeks later Argentina surrendered.

The victory made Margaret Thatcher even more popular. People thought she had acted bravely in defending the Falklands. Margaret Thatcher's

Conservative Party easily won the next election.

Although her methods and ideas sometimes made people angry—even those in her own party—Margaret Thatcher was elected again in 1987, making her the first British prime minister to win three elections in a row in more than 150 years!

But in 1990 there was strong disagreement within the Conservative Party about whether or not Britain would take part in a new European banking system. Margaret was forced to resign. John Major became the new party leader and prime minister.

In 1992 Margaret Thatcher once more returned to Parliament. But this time she was seated in the House of Lords. She wasn't called "Madame Prime Minister" any more, but instead "Lady Thatcher." Queen Elizabeth had made the grocer's daughter from Grantham a Baroness. It's customary to use a place name as part of a title, and Margaret chose the name of her old high school. Margaret's new name was Lady Thatcher of Kesteven. But to many, she'd always remain "The Iron Lady."

About the Author

Carol J. Perry has written many books for young people. She enjoys reading biographies of famous people, so she thought it would be interesting to write about women who have made it all the way to the top in the highly competitive field of politics.

Ms. Perry's fiction books include *13 And Loving It, My Perfect Winter, Make Believe Love, Sister vs. Sister,* and *Going Overboard.* Her nonfiction articles appear in many national magazines.

She lives with her husband Dan in Madeira Beach, Florida. She enjoys hearing from her readers. You can write her at the address at the front of this book.